THE CONFESSION
OF AUGUSTINE

Cultural Memory

in

the

Present

Mieke Bal and Hent de Vries, Editors

THE CONFESSION
OF AUGUSTINE

Jean-François Lyotard

Translated by

Richard Beardsworth

*Frontispiece and photographic work
by François Rouan*

STANFORD UNIVERSITY PRESS

STANFORD, CALIFORNIA

2000

Stanford University Press
Stanford, California
© 2000 by the Board of Trustees of the
Leland Stanford Junior University
Printed in the United States of America

The Confession of Augustine was originally published as
La Confession d'Augustin © 1998 Editions Galilée.

Assistance for the translation was provided by the French
Ministry of Culture.

Printed in the United States of America on acid-free, archival-
quality paper.

Library of Congress Cataloging-in-Publication Data
Lyotard, Jean-François.
    [Confession d'Augustin. English]
    The confession of Augustine / Jean-François Lyotard ;
frontispiece and photographic work by François Rouan ;
translated by Richard Beardsworth.
      p.   cm. — (Meridian)
    Includes bibliographical references and index.
    ISBN 0-8047-3792-4 (alk. paper)
    ISBN 0-8047-3793-2 (pbk.: alk. paper)
    1. Augustine, Saint, Bishop of Hippo. Confessiones.
I. Title. II. Meridian (Stanford, Calif.)
    BR65.A62.L9613 2000
    270.2'092—dc21
    [B]   00-022883

Forewarning

A posthumous book, but even more a book broken off.

Jean-François Lyotard was not able to finish his *Confession of Augustine*. The essay to be read here, appearing under the title chosen by him, presents scarcely half of the projected work. A reading of the notes alone, accumulated over the last years, suggests something like the work that he was envisaging. While unable to give account of this, the present edition nonetheless demonstrates a concern to guard the trace, however modest, of the overall project. Added to the drafted text, then, there is a *Notebook*, a collection of scattered elements that have nevertheless been arranged, each being of a distinct kind: *Sendings* joins two working texts, reflexive supports, as it were, preceding and accompa-

Forewarning

nying the writing of the book; *Fragments* assembles
a number of paragraphs, kept in reserve in the
penultimate manuscript, the writing of which JFL
wished to take up again and develop; *Pencil Sketch*
pertains indeed to sketches, to those first beginnings
on a page, dreamy escapades that JFL enjoyed pen-
ciling out to give greater flexibility to his writing,
but that remain of value for the argument announced in them, which he intended to develop in
further work—that of the duplicity of confessive
writing; *Fac-similes* needs no commentary.

As to the essay itself, it brings together two texts
written in the course of 1997.* The first text should
be seen as definitive and as forming the initial part
of *The Confession of Augustine.* The second, older
text was to be rewritten in the sort of tonal key that
governs the first part and to be reworked so as to fit

*The first text was given in Paris in October 1997, on the
occasion of a conference organized by the Collège International de Philosophie, under the title "The Confession of
Augustine." The second, given in Dunkerque in May 1997
for a colloquium organized by the Université du Littoral
and the Collège International de Philosophie, appeared
under the title "The Skin of the Skies" in *La Revue des
Sciences Humaines,* N° 248, entitled "Night."

Forewarning

with the part that was to follow. For JFL, to "rewrite" meant passing from one state to another, the last almost foreign to the first. He would have undoubtedly blown on the embers, heated to incandescence the choreography of voices, made more giddy the jealousy of his ventriloquist phrase. He wanted a confessive chase, the author's, as it were, faltering gait. For want of this particular "shedding," unfinished, Jean-François Lyotard wished that the second text, one that had already appeared under the title "The Skin of the Skies," be read in a version at least in tune with the first: held, then, to the curse of the address—to the pronominal, familiar "you"—broken up by the paragraph, with each quotation almost incorporated into the body of the text. We have tried to keep to his wishes, holding back as much as possible from any modification. Thus, from the first to the second text, neither repetitions nor the break in tone have been removed. They are testimony to a book that was broken off.

My thanks to friends Philippe Bonnefis, Michel Delorme, and François Rouan, who helped and worked on this edition.

DOLORÈS LYOTARD

Contents

quod non datur inpiis, sed eis, qui te gratis colunt,
quorum gaudium tu ipse es. Et ipsa est beata uita,
gaudere, ad te, de te propter te : ipsa est et n
altera. Qui autem aliam putant esse, aliud
gaudium neque ipsum uerum. Ab al'
imagine gaudii uoluntas eorum n

XXIII. **33** Non ergo cer⁺
esse beati uolunt, quonia⸴
uolunt, quae sola uit⸱
beatam uolunt.
caro conc⸴
ritus
u⸴

à toi
de toi,
par toi.

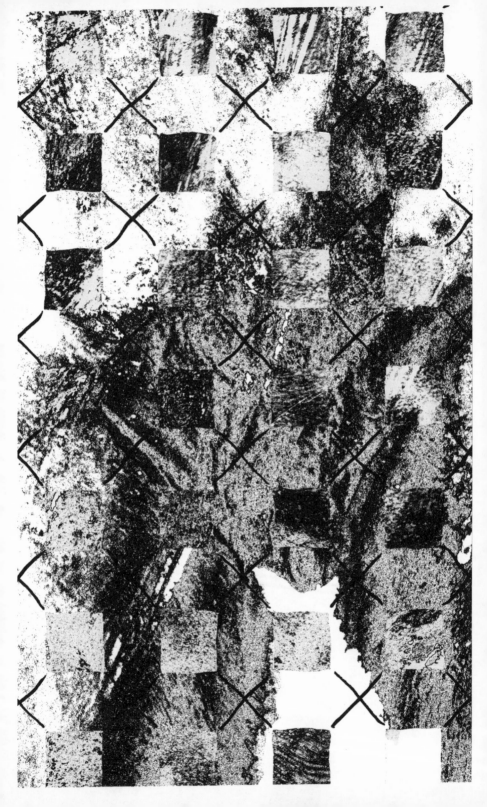

Our body with its weight strives toward its own place. Weight makes not downward only, but to its own place also. The fire mounts upward, a stone sinks downward. . . . My weight is my love; by that am I carried, whithersoever I be carried. We are inflamed by thy gift and are carried upward: we wax hot within, and we go on.

    —Augustine

THE CONFESSION OF AUGUSTINE

Blazon

Thou calledst and criest aloud to me; thou even breakedst open my deafness: thou shinest thine beams upon me, and hath put my blindness to flight: thou didst most fragrantly blow upon me, and I drew in my breath and I pant after thee; I tasted thee, and now do hunger and thirst after thee; thou didst touch me, and I even burn again to enjoy thy peace.* X, xxvii

Here, in the middle of book X, we have been hearing him complain, he has been listening to himself groan, has continued to moan, has apologized, has accused himself for being late, for always being behind you. For being delay in person, for never being on time for the encounter with you. He has been accusing you a little: you left me by the wayside, why did you abandon me? The late

---

*Augustine's *Confessions* (two volumes), trans. William Watts, Loeb Classical Library, Harvard U.P., Cambridge, Ma./William Heinemann, London: 1989 [1912]. The translation will be revised where deemed appropriate in accordance with the Latin and the French. Reference has also been made to R.S. Pine-Coffin's translation of the *Confessions* (Penguin, London: 1961). —Tr. note.

ones' lamentation, confessing their distraction, they beg to be given another chance.

O thou Beauty, how late came I to love thee, both so ancient and so fresh, yea how late came I to love thee. But behold, thou wert within me, and I out of myself, where I made search for thee: I ugly rushed headlong upon those beautiful things thou hast made. Thou indeed wert with me; but I was not with thee. These beauties kept me far enough from thee: even those, which unless they were in thee, should not be at all.

IBID.

Infatuated with earthly delights, wallowing in the poverty of satisfaction, the I was sitting idle, smug, like a becalmed boat in a null agitation. Then—but when?—you sweep down upon him and force entrance through his five estuaries. A destructive wind, a typhoon, you draw the closed lips of the flat sea toward you, you open them and turn them, unfurling, inside out.

Thus the lover excites the five mouths of the woman, swells her vowels, those of ear, of eye, of nose and tongue, and skin that stridulates. At present he is consumed by your fire, impatient for the return to peace that your fivefold ferocity brings him.

Thine eye seekest us out, he protests, it piercest

2

the lattice of our flesh, thou strokedst us with thy voice, we hasten on thy scent like lost saluki hounds. Thou art victorious; open-mouthed he gapes at your XIII, xv beatitude, you took him as a woman, cut him through, opened him, turned him inside out. Placing your outside within, you converted the most intimate part of him into his outside. And with this exteriority to himself, yours, an incision henceforth from within, you make your saint of saints, *penetrale meum*, he confesses, thy shrine in me.

The flesh, forced five times, violated in its five senses, does not cry out, but chants, brings to each assault rhythm and rhyme, in a recitative, a *Sprechgesang*. Athanasius, bishop of Alexandria, invented the practice, from what Augustine says, for the Psalms to be read in this way, a modulation of respectful voices, in the same pitch of voice, to whose accents the community of Hebrews swayed.

The Inner Human

But is the poem of the five torments a psalm? Or the blazon of a body in ecstasy? The flesh tempers fright, cushions the shattering visit that converts it into its truth. Does the flesh have an idea of this shedding of skin, an idea that this shedding reveals its true being? It has no means to think; it feels. It feels, in one, agony and joy. The most repugnant and the sweetest Christian mystery, infinity made flesh, bread and wine, is accomplished without the concept, next to the flesh, in a convulsion. This spasm is the sole witness of grace. It cannot be submitted as evidence to the tribunal of ideas, which declines comment: confession does not come under its jurisdiction.

The verse concerning the theme of your visit relates it to the past perfect. Was it the first, the only one? Has it passed? This tense in Latin, *rupisti*, you have broken up, you break up, *fugasti*, you have chased away, you chase away, can also hold for the present. A fore-echo, at the beginning of book X, has anticipated the event. In like manner the stretto in a contrapuntal piece can imitate the theme before this theme is entirely laid out, overturning the order of consequents.

The announcement here describes before the event the after-event of your fivefold assault, point by point and in perfect congruence with it. Before

and after collapse, a trait common to all violent
affection. The shrine that you have set up in the
most intimate part of his person is not a conse-
quence of your visit. The ecstatic pleasure provided
by it, that it constitutes, has no history. This is how
he speaks of it:

Whenas I love my God, I love a certain kind of
light, and a kind of voice, and a kind of fragrance,
and a kind of meat, and a kind of embrace—
embrace, taste, fragrancy, voice and light which are
of the inner human in me, *interioris hominis mei*:
where that light shineth into my soul there no
space can receive, where that voice soundeth there
no time is taken, where that fragrancy exhales there
no wind scatters; where that meat tasteth there eat-
ing devours not, and there the embrace clingeth to
me that satiety divorceth not. What I love whenas
I love my God, this is it, *hoc est*.   X, VI

May the soul, the soul-flesh, be thrown out,
smitten enough, taken from within, thrown in,
inconvenient, free of its aesthetic composure, no
more space, no more time, no more limits to sensi-
bility, to sensuality! The assault that bears down
upon the soul does not stop transfixing it. The visit
is both an encounter and not. Since the trance

never draws to an end, it did not begin. The soul,
cast out itself in its home, out of place and
moment, intrinsically, what could it place, fix, have
memorized of an avatar that abolishes the natural
conditions of perception and therefore cannot be
perceived as an event? Supposing that the syncope
takes place once or that it is repeated, how would
the soul know—since the syncope deprives the soul
of all power to gather together the diversity of
instants in a single length of time? Where can an
absolute visit be situated or placed in relation, in a
biography? How can it be related?

When it is visited, oc-cupied, in the Latin sense
of *ob-*, seized by and turned toward what falls
upon it, the soul-flesh passes into a phantom
state. It invites a fairy-story, a fable, not a discourse. Augustine's *stilus*, to be in keeping with
vibrant weakness, bends to the *timbres*, the movement of assonance and dissonance, the rhythms of
poetry. Coming from the farthest Near East,
reaching out to us, to Rimbaud, through the
courtly *canto*, the ancient figure of the erotic blazon lends itself to words, that they may confess
holy copulation.

Witness

Not memory, then, but the said inner human, who is neither man nor inner, woman and man, an outside inside. This is the only witness of the presence of the Other, of the other of presence. A singular witness, the poem. The inner human does not bear witness to a fact, to a violent event that it would have seen, that it would have heard, tasted, or touched. It does not give testimony, it is the testimony. It is the vision, the scent, the listening, the taste, the contact, each violated and metamorphosed. A wound, an ecchymosis, a scar attests to the fact that a blow has been received, they are its mechanical effect. Signs all the more trustworthy since they do not issue from any intention or any arbitrary inscription: they vouch for the event since they remain after it. Augustine's *Treatises* abound in these analyses of semiotic value: the present object evokes the absent one, in its place.

The inner human does not evoke an absence. It is not there for the other; it is the Other of the there, who is there, there where light takes place without place, there where sound resounds without

duration, and so forth. Explosive and implosive, it
is the *plosum*, the plosion canceling the *a priori*
forms of inscription and hence of possible testimony. A witness in proportion to there being none,
and there can be no witness of this blow that, we
repeat, abolishes the periods, the surfaces of the
archive. The tables of memory fall to dust, the blow
has not passed. The inner human attests *ab intestat.*

A present oxymoron, in one blow a serene erection and a tumultuous abyss, what was taken for
life dies in it, and from out of this death there
shines forth true life: *coruscasti*, you have shone,
you shine. This classic inversion of the dead and
the living weaves its motif through the whole of
the *Confessions,* as is the case in the writing of the
revelation, in the Psalms, Exodus, Genesis, in John
and Paul.

I was tarrying, Augustine confesses in book VIII,
the very moment that the repeated words *Tolle,
lege, tolle, lege,* take up and read, borne by a child's
voice from some neighbor's house, will decide for
him what he wants, I was still tarrying, dying unto
death or living unto life. He was hesitating before
the abyss of elation.

X, xxvii

VIII, xii

8

Cut

Conversion, reversion, inversion, or perversion, however one wishes to speak of it, it is a shedding of flesh, the body is suddenly transformed into soul-flesh. When I asked the appearances of the world, they replied: we are not God, he made us. But that, I the inner human, the soul, I learnt it *per sensus corporis mei*, through the senses of the body and the ministry of the outer human. With X, VI this body being punctured and penetrated by the other sense, the soul can assume bodily form, be incarnated, flesh find its soul, your presence reside in the inner human. I sought thee with my animal body, it labored, *laborans, aestans*, foamed, starved of the true. I fed the brute spadefuls of hunger-stoppers, morsels of nonsense, heresies, the fabrications of pagan theater, the masquerades of the Manichaean sect. I rolled with it into the depths of gullibility. And yet, thou, thou wert more inside me than my inmost part, *interior intimo meo*, higher than the topmost part that I could reach, *superior summo meo*. III, VI

The meeting overturns the natural seat of the

body, exceeds its great axis at both extremities, origin and head. But this is still little. In truth, the blow is a *cut*, in the sense of n-dimensional space theory. An n-dimensional space-time folds around the naturally three-dimensional volume of the body: what would cut into the latter body, a plane for example, which indeed separates two regions of space, loses this property when inserted into four-dimensional space. Its function becomes that of a line in ours or that of a point in a plane, either of which cut nothing.

To conceive the logic of these transformations of space, Augustine cannot rely on Dedekind and Poincaré geometry. For want of this, seeking to represent to himself how you, Lord, are present at your creation, he has the following image: the totality of bodies, including those places occupied by pure spirits if they were bodies, forms one very great mass, as big as I thought convenient, for I could not come to the knowledge of its true expanse, a mass in every part surrounded and penetrated by thee, *ex omni parte ambientem et penetrantem eam*, for thou art infinite in whatever aspect thou art grasped. It is, he adds, as if there were supposed to be a sea, which everywhere and on every side by a

most unmeasurable infiniteness should only be a
sea; and that sea should contain in it some huge
sponge, but yet finite; which sponge must needs be
everywhere and on every side filled by that unmeasurable sea.   VII, v

Such is flesh visited, co-penetrated by your
space-time, disturbed and confused with this blow,
but steeped in infinity, impregnated and pregnant
with your overabundant liquid: the waters of the
heavens, he says. The body, sponge-like in its per-
meability to the other space-time, exceeds its *senso-
ria*. Lifted are the blindness waiting for vision from
the other side of the visual field, the deafness at the
edge of hearing, the anorexia threatening taste, the
anosmia smell, and the anesthesia touch. If the
human, thus bestowed with grace, is declared to be
inner, it is simply because the secret of such an
ecstasy remains kept, because the words to express
it are lacking. Not easily does grace let itself be
revealed.

The confessing I looks for words and, contrary
to all expectation, those that come to him are those
that make physiology work to the point of pushing
the body's sensorial and hence sensual powers to
the infinite. The inhibition that naturally overtakes

him is lifted, it is metamorphosed into generosity. To deliver the soul from its misery and death, grace does not demand a humiliated, mortified body; rather, it increases the faculties of the flesh beyond their limits, and without end. The ability to feel and to take pleasure unencumbered, pushed to an unknown power—this is saintly joy.

Grace rarely takes a less dialectical turn, less negativist, less repressive. In Augustine, flesh bestowed with grace fulfills its desire, in innocence.

Resistance

Does this mean to say that everything is accomplished, felicity procured with the inner human, life forever vouching for true life? Has the sinner jumped, bags and all, onto the other side of the firmament? Has the dreadful delay that makes the creature run after its truth in vain been filled in, has the accursed time in which the encounter with the absolute is incessantly put off been abolished? No, the pagan, at thirty-two years of age, indeed later, has not finished taking his cup of pleasure as the sun shines and the snows fall on the Aures; not finished either with the games he played with friends in Thagaste, with the rhetorical exploits at Hippon or Carthage, and with the drinking bouts; and he has by no means finished with seducing pretty girls and mounting his mistress. For appetite is resistant, in the tense body of the African, a pebble polished by the wind, tanned by the sun, broken in to racing, ball games, and the ways of the bed. And indefatigable remains the rhetor's concupiscence for argument and persuasion, forever vivacious in Rome, Milan, and again at Cassiciacum when, after the said conversion, he retired from the practice of law. Sure of their means as they are, indifferent to their ends, muscle stiffens against the Other's hold, neck refuses to let pass the word that is not its own.

What a scandal, the other flesh, the other voice parasiting his own voices, what an aversion, the conversion! His body and speech, brought up to dominate and to exude sensuality, do not bend unprotesting to a regime whose *rex* is not of him and whose rule lies beyond his grasp. The course of real life, biography, gives lasting resistance to the improbable event of your coming.

At the end of the book of hours page after page
of which the will runs out of breath from confiding
itself to the Other, that his will be done, the very
last words of the *Confessions* repeat, hammer out in
vain the promise. For they still exhale the bitterness
of the unaccomplished:

Thou being the Good, needing no good, art at
rest always, because thy rest thou art thyself. And
what man is he that can teach another man to
understand this? Or what angel, another angel? Or
what angel, man? Let it be begged of thee, be sought
in thee, knocked for at thee; so shall it be received,
so shall it be found, and so shall it be opened.

XIII, xxxviii

You will open your door, it will be crossed, entry
will be had, for certain, it's a promise—for those at
least who are of the elect. But it is for tomorrow, it
still lies in the future, one has to be dead already,
once time is over.

On the point of resting his *stilus* after thirteen
books of contrition and celebration of grace incar-
nate, the penitent finds himself on the threshold of
your door, still stuck in the thick pall of affairs,
pulling in every direction on the harness of the
before, of the after—wishes, sorrows, pleasures. He
has aged in vain, the young master, the brilliant

seducer, old in matters of devotion, an eye always watching the seeds of evil growing everywhere. It is as if, encysted within the folds of the bishop's holy soul, the sexual—for it is it—turns out to be of such stamina that, next to it, the small change of chance encounters of ecstasy, the parsimony of secret meetings with the Other count for nothing.

You will not have brought the stray one to your step, a step that never advances. Futile history continues, the world of death is not dead. The other time, without duration, the other field without horizon, yours, cannot be measured by the *gnômon*, the compass of living creatures. As your years do not end, your years are always the day of today. But thou art the same still. And all tomorrows and so forward, and all yesterdays and so backward, thou shalt make present in this day of thine; yea, and hast made present.   I, VI

Distentio

It is scarcely as if the assault of your eternity signs itself, with a syncope, with what is, after all, a nothing, in the calendar of days. A tiny wing, come from elsewhere, brushes him very lightly with your presence, it does not take him away from the concerns of his dead life. Your visitation is almost indiscernible when compared to the slow beat of habit and the dissipation of desire.

The euphoria of a drunken beggar encountered in the street, Ambrose, his open door, him reading in silence, the fresh voice from the neighboring house reaching the fig tree in the Milanese garden where Augustine cries prostrate on the ground— this makes for a highly discreet, not to say impish, signaling of the absolute. These few signs, threaded within the tissue of the things of life, are rarely made out by him, and certainly never immediately, as signs with a calling value, smoothly coated in the facile evidence of reality.

Only after the event, when the uneasiness will have prevailed, when the worry of having gone astray concerning the direction of his life will have driven him to scrutinize the past in order to tear from its loquacious silence what this past perhaps meant, or means for him now, only then, through memory, or rather through anamnesis, will he recompose the hidden semiotics bestrewing his history. Yet he will have been blind, hurriedly thrown, without him knowing, onto paths unbeknown to him, right to the end.

Strange misrecognition, a distraction, a leading astray more essential, more archaic than your truth, one might say. For time itself, the time of living creatures, the time that he calls created, is the child of this permanent self-absence. To go blank is what we say for a lapse in memory, but what falls out into the three temporal instances is the oblivion inherent to existence itself. Past, present, future—as many modes of presence in which the lack of presence is projected.

The delay that throws the confessing I into despair is not due to a failure in its chronology; no, *chronos*, at once and in its entirety, consists in delay. Even the shattering visit of the Other, even the incarnation of grace, if it ever truly arrives, from the fact that this visit subverts the space-time of the creature, it does not follow that it removes this creature from the hurried, limp course of regrets, remorse, hope, responsibilities, from the ordinary worries of life.

But it is even worse than that. Delighting with your presence in such sudden ecstasy, he feels more in dissociation from himself, cleaved, alienated, more uncertain of what he is than usual. But thou, O Lord my God, hearken, behold and pity and heal me, thou in whose eyes I am now become a question to myself, *mihi quaestio factus sum et ipse est languor meus*, and that is my languor.

X, xxxiii

Lagaros, languid, bespeaks in Greek a humor of limpness, a disposition to: What's the point? Gesture relaxes therein. My life, this is it: *distentio*, letting go, stretching out. Duration turns limp, it is its nature. But more so from the fact or phantasm of the Other's visit. The everyday ego tries willy-nilly to gather the dispersion of what befalls it under the unity of a single history. Broken, sundered by the blow of your encounter, it grows anxious: Where am I, who am I? And the languor lulls to sleep the straying of a: But, after all, so what?

XI, xxix

The Sexual

The endurance of the sexual is its *flaccidity*. It bends, it slips, it does not confront. Its flights of anger are, precisely, flights. The sexual is not subjected to time, if Freud is to be believed, and on occasions dispatches in its course offspring who disorganize it and are remarked within it. Augustine's confession is still inspired by another motif which, together with the preceding trait, confers upon the power of the sexual a more fearful inconsistency, that of structuring the entire course of experience. A-temporal as it is, enemy as it is of chronological order, this powerless power would also be, so to speak, the agent, the bearer of what is recurrently deferred, making the triple instance of time, or temporal existence, what it is: the not yet, the already no longer and the now. From book XI of the *Confessions* Husserl reads off the phenomenology of the internal consciousness of time. In this book Augustine sketches out from below a libidinal-ontological constitution of temporality.

The sexual continuously surprises, takes from behind, works from the back. Upright resolutions, probity and the honest promise—the sexual lets all this go; it will pass. Somnolence is its accomplice, much stronger than vigilance. Representations, *imagines*, lascivious things, fixed by sheer habit, if they assail me when I am awake, they are without force, but when I am asleep, they take me off into pleasure and, what is more, to consenting to pleasure and to experiencing it, as if it were real. So powerful is the error induced in the soul and in the flesh by these images that the scene which, feigned in sleep, seduces me is unable to do so when I am awake. Does that mean, the confessing I worries, that I am X, xxx   not myself, O Lord my God, when sleeping?

The other of the I, the *ipse*, is indeed awake when I sleep. But is not thine hand that can do all, he pleads, able to cure the languor, *sanare languores*, of my soul, *lascivos motus mei soporis extinguire*, and IBID.   quench the lascivious motions of my sleep. Sleep does not belong to I. Another principle, another prince exercises at its own pace on the stage of the dream the languorous and lascivious illusions. When the master's lieutenant, controlling the passions and upright in chastity, is on leave, what can the master do? Has he not given the conjurer the reins?

So great is the sovereignty of artifices that the dreamer has trouble distinguishing them from dreams that you have sent him. Monica, the mother, was so happy to be able to tell, from whatever relish it was, she said, which she could not put into words, those dreams where your presence was VI, xiii   revealed from those of her own spirit. Happy are

they, he exclaims, who, seized by an unexpected motivation, contrary to every rule, know that it was thou who gave the command. Your signs are deci-   III, ix
phered by Monica whatever state she is in, awake or asleep. The wooden rule on which she sees herself in a dream perched with her son near, she knows it to be the rule of faith, and Augustine, then sunk in debauchery, will not fail to embrace it.   III, xi

As for him, it is not that he hears your call, he does not want to hear it. Like a sleeper after whom one urgently calls: Arise, here is true joy! And he persists in playing with his phantasies. Ears open, members deaf. A little more of not yet. The languor of the later excites the immediate.

He is told of sudden conversions: that of the very pagan Victorinus, *iam me esse christianum*, would you have said that I am already a Christian?;   VIII, ii
that of two young wolves from the entourage of the emperor—at the sight of a *Life* of Antony lying open in a wooden hut, what is one doing with one's eye still upon the favors of Valentinian, while to be the friend of God, however little I may wish it, here I am even now, *si voluero, ecce nun fio.* These edify-   VIII, vi
ing narratives reach him with clarity; misted over with the charm of the magical, they add to his

impatience, but also to his patience. He clearly
hears the Arise thou that sleepest that Paul shouted
VIII, v   at the Ephesians, but he cannot get up. Much bet-
ter were it for me to give myself up to thy charity
than to give myself over to my own covetousness,
but notwithstanding that former course pleased
and convinced me, yet this latter seized me and
IBID.   held me confined.

Two attractions, two twin appetites, almost
equal in force, what does it take for one to prevail
upon the other? A nuance, an accent, a child hum-
ming an old tune? Who speaks here of transcendence when divine grace is placed at the same level
as a charm? Evil is perhaps not substantial, as the
Manichaeans believe, just a matter of willing,
asserts the repentant, of, that is, desire. But evil is to
desire the good just as one desires evil.

Consuetudo

See, here I come, just a moment more. But the
VIII, v   moment does not pass, there is no sequel. Laziness
prevents even the deciphered signs from being put

22

to work, a sluggishness concerning change, which he names *consuetudo*, the quietude of *ipse* close to *ipse*. A stagnant energy, *lex enime peccati est violentia consuetudinis*, since the law of sin is the violence of custom, a law without law, the customary law of what is done, what has always already been done.

It is neither that concupiscence balks at undergoing too severe a treatment, nor that it is threatened by the practice of faith with an awesome castration, in the manner of Tertullian's radicalism. No, the taste of pleasure can find its happiness in the Christic *caritas*. And the blazon has made us hear with what stunning sensual exultation—phantasized or real, where is the difference if one is used to sleeping?—, with what ecstatic pleasure is enacted the rape perpetrated by the Other. This ravishment is also undergone in surprise, there is no need to get to one's feet, to confront the Other head on, to experience the delights of torment— rather, the contrary.

To the being lying down in custom nothing must happen but from the back. Just as he is on the verge of agreeing to get up, the old girlfriends, the amusing toys, the adorable vanities pull him back, hold him fast: And shall we no longer accompany thee from

IBID.

23

The Confession of Augustine

this time for ever? And what were those things which they suggested to me in that phrase this or that? This and that, O my God, you know well, he entreats, what impurities, *sordes*, what most shameful things, *dedecora*, did they suggest to me, muttering as it were **VIII, xi** softly behind my back, *a dorso mussitantes*. As if, he feigns believe, they wanted him to turn around toward them. Nothing of the sort, however—he and they are used to being taken by surprise, only to being themselves by surprise, for dirty habits have no need of a contract, they are contracted *a tergo*. With *consuetudo violenta*, the custom of being violated by custom, turpitude is so violent that it need only murmur: Thinkest thou to be ever able to live with-
IBID. out all that?—women, concubines, the unclean world of the other sex, it takes but a faint whisper to keep him on the bed a little while longer.

Concupiscence waits for it to be too late, temp-tation lingers on, pleasure will come in a cata-strophic rush, the I will have been able to do noth-ing to ward off the rout. This future anterior in the negative sets the future upon a powerlessness that is always already accomplished. And the *ipse* com-fortably nestles its fatigue into this time of lifeless relapse. Giving itself up to it, in the course of

24

The Confession of Augustine

Augustine writing, the *ipse* eludes the cruelty of a real beginning, of adieus, of fright.

The *ipse* is unable to face the adventure of an unknown future, to envisage it in itself, by itself, for itself. Sedentary. The *ipse* ought at least to be wrung out, to be shown its behind from the front, completely naked, abject, presented to the horrified look of uprightness. While listening to the story of Ponticianus that tells of the conversion of ambitious courtiers, Augustine experiences, he says, the inverse torture, that of being pulled up straight. Lifted up from his back while asleep, he is cast straightaway before his own eyes: turpid, unsound, sordid, bespotted, ulcerous, the arse of a turned-over carrion, a sight to be abhorred. The Lord's grip holds him fast, with his nose over the filth, that he may loathe it, that he may decide to flee that self, *ipse*, and cast off the moorings, bound for you.

In vain, however. Yet again the straightening effect that the example of the true departure was meant to create soon fades, however tormenting it was; it is cushioned, absorbed within the elasticity of the constant return to the same. It is not, he says, that I had not known my infamy, I had dissembled it, had winked at it, and forgotten it.   VIII, VII

25

Oblivion

Oblivion, the great concern of the *Confessions*, if it is true that to confess has as task to hide nothing any longer, to shed light upon what has remained crouched in the night of life, and to offer it up and return it to you, the giver. At the beginning of the fifth book: Receive here the sacrifice of my confessions, *de manu linguae meae*, from the hand of my tongue which thou hast formed and stirred up to confess unto thy name. In true sacrifice, the confession gives back to him who first gave and gives forever. In the event, the reciprocity of roles appears so close that the writer leaves unsettled whether it is he, the sacrificer, who is the author of the offering, or you. If your Word or his tongue will have written these memoirs. He will not know, and you are silent.

V, 1

Since to confess is to bring into language, to language what eludes language, the object to be sacrificed, the most precious possession one has, as must be the case, is here silence. To confess explicitly to that which has said nothing and says nothing, to give what one has not been, what one is not, is the exorbitant work to which Augustine harnesses himself: a working-through, we would say today.

It is, then, childhood that is brought first to the altar, which not having the use of linguistic signs, *in-fantia*, has left no traces for which I can answer before you. For what have I to do with it, whereof I can no vestige recall to memory? Beginnings absolutely unknown, conception, uterine life, birth, breastfeeding, crib-rage, senseless gesticulations, jealousy toward the suckling-brother at the breast, this period of my life that I did not live, and that has been reported to me.

I, VII

Is it a sin? It is the sin of time, delay. The encounter with the act is missed from the beginning. The event comes before writing bears witness, and writing sets down once the event has passed. Confession reiterates this condition of childhood measured against the scale of full presence: I will have always been small with regard to your greatness. You, you who had no childhood, you are not transported into the oscillations of too soon and too late. Thus forms, infantile, the imago of the perfectly erect, pure act, word absolved from

antecedent and consequent. The little one honors
the great one with tiny names, with *hoc*, with *id*,
with *id ipsum*, this, that, that itself: that—a deictic
without object, bearing in ontology the name of
that which has none, eponym, anonym.

VII, xvii; IX, x;
X, vi; XII, vii

The small child undertakes to learn and make
known what he does not know, confident, with
Matthew, that it is to little children that thou hast
revealed, and from the learned that thou hast hidden. Confession is written posthumously, in search
of the *anthume*, in *distentio* then. And *distentio*
recurs, returns in the quick of confessive writing.
The delay that this writing seeks to fill in, to retrace
through running after you, through running after
the act—this delay is not to be caught up. The very
time taken for the proclamation of the instant of
your actuality to be written down, the time taken
to go through the delay again, to obtain pardon for
misspent time, the raised hand of pagan seques-
tration, the pardon for heresy, absolution for debauchery—confession aggravates the belatedness of
this time lost in gaining time over time.

VII, ix

Is the confessing I innocent in all this?—Is there
not a little pleasure afforded in deferring, in squan-

dering, in diverting urgency into childish pursuits?
The great wealth of style deployed in petitions and
celebrations, the courtly figures of speech dispensed in abundance with the pretext of persuad-
ing a judge who has no need of persuasion (since
he already knows all there is to know), the flowers
of poetry sampled here and there, the falsely wise
arguments aiming to give substance to a meta-
physics that is, after all, nothing but a hazardous
allegoric and one, what is more, that is lax in its
interpretation—one is led to suspect that such
decorous language, a language so full of pathos, is
yielding to the pleasure of length, to its being
drawn out, to the languor found in the very
avowal of the sin of languor. From behind his
back, as ever, the old young female partners in sin,
dispensers of this and that, murmur to their
denouncer the supreme vanity—to play the great
writer. Of scorning vainglory, he brazenly writes,
one can provide oneself glory all the more vainly.   X, xxxvii
What a way, indeed, of asserting the fact that he is
worth nothing! He had to write to save himself
from oblivion, and yet through writing he forgets
himself . . .

Temporize

But, all the same, will it be said, memory is his main weapon against forgetfulness? One can even remember having forgotten, he remarks. Before reviewing each concupiscence, he sets out in book X to explore the vast *praetoria* of memory, its palaces, its treasures. He draws up a systematic inventory of memories stocked on the shelf, each by category: images of corporal sensations, catalogued according to which sense, easily available; then, a little to one side, but retrievable through study, the elements of thought, its tools, the problems, the notions; finally *affectiones*, the affects, which memory retains but, like a stomach that holds its food, deprived of taste. The memory of a joy is not joyous, emotion is something actual, nothing is retained from it but the tasteless occurrence. That the affective quality is lost is at least not lost.

What is the balance of this inventory: that memory is solid, trustworthy, that it is in truth the mind itself, all *animus*? Not at all. He comments: memory, what energy it has, what energy it is! It exceeds my forces, those of me, the ego, it is a field of

X, xvi

hindrances and sweat from my labor, something horrifying, folds upon folds, dens of them, innumerable, a life so various, so full of changes, vehemently immense, *immensa vehementer.* I turn and IBID. flit about from one to another, mining into them as far as I am able, and *finis nusquam*, and there is no end in sight, nowhere. So great is the energy of memory, so great the energy of life, he concludes, in this man who lives of mortal life, *in homine vivente mortaliter.*   X, XVII

These last words say it: the overall balance is actually disastrous. The I can try as it likes to reassure itself, putting finishing touches to the lucid taxonomy of memories. The contents of memory, however, all that can happen to the *ipse* in the course of life, reverberate with a chaotic dynamic that condenses, displaces, topples over their images into each other, disfigures them endlessly. Behind the guardian of time, supposed to watch over its order, under the wing of memory, the work of the drives persists in turning languid the seizure of events. The clear phenomenology of internal temporality covers over a strange mechanic, a grammar of the ways in which concupiscence conjugates essential frustration.

It is not of the mind itself, as it is written, *ipsius animi*, that time turns out to be a threefold *distentio* but, within the mind, of the desire that bears three XI, xxvi times the mourning of its thing. When he expects it, *expectat*, the *distentio* pre-poses and proposes to come; when he seeks to apprehend it, by dint of attention, *adtendit*, it is ex-posed and supposed in the present; when he gives it to himself in such a way that it is retained, *meminit*, it is deposed and reposes XI, xxviii in the past. These object positions are never posed, but indisposed, apt to slip away, since dis-propriation gives them birth. The object is only there to the extent that it is not there, it passes in transit, its present nickname does nothing but streak with the tiniest of flashes the interface between two clouds of nonexistence, the not yet and the already no longer. Impatience, boredom, haste, or suffering lengthens time, pleasure or surprise shortens it. Time is measured by *affectio*, in the singular mode in which things touch us in their eclipse, *affectio quam res* XI, xxvii *praetereuntes in nos faciunt.*

The *ipse* shall not have, does not have, and did not have what it desires. It lacks being, and drugs its privation in temporal mode. It lives a mortal life, it survives, outlives itself, arranges it such that it is never on time for its objects, it *temporizes*. Temporality is its settling down, to *ipse*, its way of getting on with the unaccomplished, with custom, with the deferment of the act. The times decline deception, time bows and relinquishes presence.

Immemorable

And the Other, then, the true? You, where does he find your trace in this disorder of muffled deceptions? He reasons thus: time is disastrous? But, precisely, the essential frustration that gives birth to him receives his seed with a constant, universal appetite, one that does not tolerate laziness, that is uncompromising toward any transaction: the desire to be happy. Now you alone, being perfect, can give the *vita beata*. *Gaudere, ad te, de te, propter te*, to rejoice concerning thee unto thee and for thy sake: this is the happy life, and there is no other. He   X, xxii
encounters, or believes he encounters, this mad, perfect joy when you come to visit him, crushing his skin and soul. But, then, who is he at that

moment, what is that that he loves when he loves his god? Does he remember?

The I that holds the *comput* of his life asserts its rights: the memory of the perfect does indeed figure, he claims, in the archive. See now, how many spaces I have run over in my memory seeking thee, Lord; and I found thee not outside it. For I find nothing at all concerning thee but what I have kept in memory, ever since I first learnt thee: for, he insists, he swears it is so, I have never forgotten thee, since the time I first learnt thee. Since therefore I learnt to know thee, hast thou always kept in my memory; and there still do I find thee, whenever I call thee to remembrance, and delight myself in thee.

Note, however, the restriction: from the moment that you were known to me. The avowal is enough for the soul-flesh to appeal to the authority of the mind: where, then, did I find thee that I might learn thee? The soul-flesh objects: For in my memory thou wert not before I learnt thee! And concludes: In what place therefore did I find thee, that so I might learn thee, in what place but *in te super me*, in thee, far above me? Supposing that the mind could have miraculously kept trace of an

X, xxiv

X, xxvi

Ibid.

encounter that does not take place in its place or time, its memory would still be worth nothing. Just as the succulence of a morsel of meat held in the mouth is lost when digested by the stomach, conscious memory would, at best, only retain from the encounter an episode purged of the formidable emotion that metamorphoses flesh and soul.

How would such a *memorandum*, without body, testify to the presence of the Other? Not upon the standing of the I, well-trained to think, nor in the soft tissue of the spongy *ipse*, but in those *vacuomes* full of you, in you, then, on the hybrid edge that you weave, in a web of sophistry, for me above my head; there alone you fall upon me, you despoil me, you transport me away. True life, happiness jump like flying fishes in my lapses of memory, pockets for your ocean, breaks in the clouds for your sky.

Differend

Dissidio, dissensio, dissipatio, distensio, despite wanting to say everything, the I infatuated with putting its life back together remains sundered, separated from itself. Subject of the confessive work, the first person author forgets that he is the work of writing. He is the work of time: he is waiting for himself to arrive, he believes he is enacting himself, he is catching himself up; he is, however, duped by the repeated deception that the sexual hatches, in the very gesture of writing, postponing the instant of presence for all times.

You, the Other, pure verb in act, life without remainder, you are silent. If he encounters you, the I explodes, time also, without trace. He calls that "god" because that is the custom of the day, theology also being a work of custom. And, here, the differend is such, between your vertiginous visitation and thinking, that it would be as smug as the last, as false and as deceptive, to explain that not the name of god, but that itself, *id ipsum*, far above me, the mad joy, proceeds from the sexual. Who can take the common measure of something incommensurable? A form of knowledge that vaunts that it can do so, in bestriding the abyss, forgets the abyss and relapses. The cut is primal.

The Confession of Augustine

Firmament

Is it not true that you dispensed the skin of the skies like a book?

And who except thou, O our God, made that firmament of the authority of the divine Scripture to be over us? For the sky shall be folded up like a book, and is even now stretched over us like a skin.   XIII, xv

The day of your wrath: Isaiah announces with what calamities the fury of Yahweh will strike the Edomites and all the accursed nations with it. Their slain shall be left unburied, stink shall spread up out of the rotting corpses, the mountains shall melt with blood, and the heavens, adds the prophet, shall be rolled up like a scroll. Then beasts will establish forever on the devastated land their   *Isaiah*, XXXIV, reign of wildness.   3-4

The mantle of fur that you stretch out like a canopy over our heads is made from animal skin, the same clothing that our parents put on after they had sinned, the coverings of the exiled, with which to travel in the cold and the night of lost lives, sleepwalkers stumbling to their death.

Curses, also, of divine anger through the inheritance of the first fault, condemned to die from birth, *generatione*, as our ancestors were after the initial banishment, we also, we, forever, have to endure the mantle of skin. It betokens the condition of mortality, *mortalitas*. Humans share with wild beasts the destiny of extinction.

Enarr. in Ps.
CIII, 1

The scroll of salvation is rolled.

And yet, the night that extinguishes us, suspended over our eyes, is not irrevocable like that of beasts. The skin whose lattice prevents clear sight covers the spine of a book that is folded up, that is perhaps inside out. Our sky, undecipherable as it is made by the shadow that overcasts our eyes, does not carry all the less, on the side turned toward us, the signs of your writing. One imagines the book cover bound in skin branded with letters. For the firmament that you throw out above us as a curse also announces your promise.

Author

Is it not thou and thou alone, O our God, so demands the confessant, is it not thou who has made us that firmament of authority of thy divine scripture to be over us? *Firmament,* a firm support—this is what the sky of skin also constitutes, the support of a breviary dedicated by the author to the edification of mortal beings. A writing sparkles under the vault of the skies, the glow of the verb in our bestial half-light. This streak of light, far from growing weak, appears all the more bright, its intensity all the more "sublime" since the great mortals, your servants who have given us the eternal script, have died out.

For this book remains, while, one after the other, Moses, David, John, and Paul, who came to spread and augment the word of the Holy, have disappeared. The ephemeral being of their life highlights *a contrario* the perpetuity of your message as well as its increase. *Auctoritas* is the faculty of growing, of founding, of instituting, of vouchsafing. Majestic is its superlative state. Nothing has this power that has the writing of the creator, no firmament can stretch out more firm above its creatures than the archivolt of the text of the Immutable. Your signature comes and appends itself, vouchsafes itself on the vault of the world. You are the author.

The immortal initials mortal creation; its seal is

established thereupon as the vault protects the church.

And yet, we from below, we scarcely read these signs that are still too high, still too dazzling. In like manner, birds of the night, barn owls, screech owls take fright, with their nictitating eyelids, a third skin, an added layer of film, lowering over their pupils, without impairing sight, so as to protect against the full shock of the sun. Little is it to say that the eyes of your creatures blink, they are veiled, adapted to the night of sin, they decipher in bits. We mumble our way through the traces left by the absolute that you are; we spell the letters.

In truth, Augustine explains, we read because we do not know how to read. To the children of sin, the word reaches them obscured, and the supreme light from which it emanates is absorbed into our eyes in episodic flashes, in these precarious moments of clarity whose successive appearance, like linear sequences of discourse, we pursue. The true book is closed to us, the book of your truth, one in face-to-face, all at once.

Undoubtedly, if we saw and heard the dazzling clamor of your wisdom without any filter, if we received it all at once, it would contort our faces, would unfix the orbit of our eyes, would turn us into a white-hot firebrand, subsiding quickly into ashes. The book in the form of the firmament filters the formidable presence of the author. Chased out of the paradise of your intimacy, we are left for memory by you the collection of your works, the world, a text of which we form as much a part as its readers. Decipherable decipherers, in the library of shadows.

Angels

Augustine dreams of the other one: above the canopy of skin, on a second level of your creation, I know that another reign lies open, immense, bathed in light, where what you are thinking is read quite otherwise. The library of angels is to be found in the waters of the above, beyond the firmament. There emanates from the super-celestial numbers that people it a continual hymn of praise to you: unheard-of canticles, silence.

The angelic beings have no need, like us, to gaze up at the enigmas of this firmament, and by read-

ing to attain the knowledge of thy Word. For they always behold thy face, and there do they read, without any syllables measurable by time, what the
XIII, xv meaning is of thy eternal will. O marvel, wonderful act of reading, without mediation. The very thought of the author, in pure love. *Lectio, electio, dilectio*: they are forever reading, and that never passes away which they read. They read the immutable—can one call this reading?—in an im-
IBID. mutable way. Is it not said of a lover that he "reads" the emotion that moves across the face of his beloved? Similarly, it suffices for the angels to behold thy face to understand it. It conceals nothing within itself, nor anything that will change. A presence of which we have no idea, an infinite ocean of light without shadow. The book of the angels is never closed, nor is their scroll folded up since seeing thyself art this unto them, yea, thou art
IBID. so eternally.

Book without letter, unwritten scripture, the library of the angels is, in truth, empty. More like a "kenoary," because an "ontoary": being folds within it, but without the folding of a book. Knowing knowledge unfolds as known knowledge, as a source of light is diffused in luminous waves. For so

is the fountain of life with thee, like as in thy light
we shall see light.   XII, xvi

God only sees himself in God. Compared with
his incomparable brightness, all is night, and
speech is noise after the silence of the lauds. In the
sky of skies, the heaven of heavens, wisdom celebrates its glory. The intelligence with which the
angelic creatures are infused is not co-eternal with
their creator, but it is exempt from becoming.

Next to your perpetual today, what do our sea-
sons and days recount? The comings and goings of
a sun, prisoner of the night, held in periodic
eclipse.

Signs

And yet the letters inscribed on our sky inspire
their readers to compare incomparables. An un-
crossable divide, it seems, between the eternal and
time—through the signs that it addresses to us, the
firmament calls out to being from out of becoming, suggesting, from within the perishable, an alle-
gory of the immutable. The lower peoples gaze up

and learn thy mercy, which declares in time thee
XIII, xv   that madest times. For the sake of the salvation of
its creatures, the absolute word inflicts upon itself
the becoming of signs.

These suffer the temporal condition twofoldly:
reading plunges them in its successive course, con-
demning them thereby to an evanescent state; and,
bearing value for something other than themselves,
their deciphering and interpretation are never safe
from mistakes. Alteration holds the law over our
letters: due, first, to their temporal sequence and,
second, to their signifying value. The Augustinian
treatises, *De Magistro*, *De Dialectica*, *De Rhetorica*,
teem to obsession with marks of suspicion brought
against the validity of linguistic units.

Just think, the slightest shift of stress, a syllabic
quantity that has been missed, *léporem* instead of
leporem, and a hare presents itself when one was
expecting charm. And words that forever run from
one nothing to the next. Augustine complains that
the present flies so rapidly from future to past that
the slightest pause is excluded, *ut nulla morula*
XI, xv   *extandatur*. So much so that none of the three
temporal states in which a sign is successively pre-

sented truly *is*. Writing tails off between two abysses.

Modern phenomenological thought has made these analyses famous. The temporal instances are not beings but modes according to which an object is presented to consciousness. Augustine says: to the mind, *spiritu*. He respectively names waiting, attention, and memory, the presence to mind of the future, of the present, and of the past. Annihilating acts of intention since they set up their object, diversely but constantly, as absent: not yet there, no longer there, and the there now of the present, ungraspable. Weak tensions in the night of nonbeing, subsiding into it.

But the confessant who is writing here is not a philosopher. A creature at work, working for its conversion, one who does not stop turning toward the true light, so fearful is it of falling into delusion, into hallucination—a creature laments the anxiety of being abandoned to the night. Temporality blows death over things and signs.

Wave of nothing breaking over wave of nothing. Augustine feels drowned, his voice begins to chant the *qînâh* and the *tehillâh*, the broken rhythm of lamentation, the vibrant tempo of celebration. He begs God to light his lamp in the darkness of this world below, in which everything, including his signs, fades and dies.

Animus

I have been written in my life, so says the confessant to himself, and I have understood nothing, forever relating anything that happens to myself, forever reading events at their face value. Even the arguments, the reasons and the causes that are articulated in philosophical or rhetorical mode by the *animus*, the intellect, even the disciplines of the mind remain immanent to the text of the world, presuming to find light in its obscurity. To climb back beyond the uncertain meanings and pierce the firmament—*animus* rebels against this wayward movement, since it would lose therein its eyes and its concepts.

It knows, conversely, how to find itself in time. Memory is its strong point, its stomach, writes Augustine, but more than that, memory *is* the mind itself. The mind stocks data in its vast stores of memory, it finds them in their place, recognizes them, and effortlessly recalls them. If it has met God, it will remember so, it will recognize him. It has all the means of time at its disposal since it is the one, with its negative-affirmative force of retaining in presence what is not there, to represent to itself absent things, to order and articulate them, to anticipate and conclude as if they made a world. It is the friend of time, with it straightforward succession is subdued. One thing upon another, for certain; but the first thing is now conserved in the second, and the second is now made pregnant with the first.

The mind proposes a dialectic with a flux, becoming bears its fruit, and secular judgment benefits from the clarity that the rewriting of thought pulls out of the disorder of lived experiences. The *Confessions* could not have been written without the competence of *animus*, the contribution of its memory together with its ability to plan an aim.

But what aim? Is it a question of recounting a life while correcting its mistakes, its errors, so as to bear witness as faithfully as possible to reality? But what reality? If it was only that, to attest, to verify what took place and be persuaded of it, *animus* would indeed do the job.

He is good at it, the boy whom Patricius, his father, as a Roman of good pagan stock, pushed into the discursive arts to turn him into the athlete that he is at argumentation, in the pretoriums and assemblies. *Narratio* is, after all, part of rhetorical discourse, indeed it is far from being the least of its moments: when the lawyer recounts the fact, true or false, he persuades. Not even to mention the passion of convincing: the schoolboy has also trained therein, he excels in the desire of philosophy, pagan or not, the desire to restore the diverse to the unity of the true through the exclusive play of logical articulation. These are the works of the *mind*.

Fissure

But the *Confessions* are not of this vein: neither a plea whose end would be mastered and fixed by virile intellect, a cause to defend or against which

to summon; nor a treatise of philosophy in which
the path would be traced through conceptual dis-
crimination between this and that, the sensible and
the intelligible, soul and body, reason and imagina-
tion. Confession does not decide, on the contrary:
a fissure zigzags across all that lends itself to writing, to the great vexation of *animus*, whose binary
clarity is humiliated. The caesura does not take
place, has not the time. The here and now, the
stretches of time, the places, the lives, and the I
present themselves as fissured, or rather, fissure
continually. The field of reality, discourse included,
fissures in its entirety, like a struck glass.

The strike of conversion is not one single blow
delivered once and for all; it is not a shower of
repeated blows either. No, confessive writing bears
the fissure along with it. Augustine confesses his
God and confesses himself not because he is converted: he becomes converted or tries to become
converted while making confession. Conversion is
the fissure in the grain of confession, it is not the
substitution of an amended, luminous version for a
blind, poor version of profane life. No longer will
there be night and day for the confessant; henceforth it is fissured day and fissured night. And it is

in the minuscule chink of this fissure that the *stilus* is styled, in the precarious, reciprocal balance of enigma and demonstration.

Animus becomes worried. Why should not memory suffice for the task of giving light to what was dark? See, O Lord, how great a space I have coursed over in my memory seeking thee; and I found thee not outside it! For I find nothing at all concerning thee, but what I have kept in memory, ever since I first learnt thee. For, since the hour I first learnt thee, I have never forgotten thee. . . . Since this time I learnt to know thee, hast thou remained in my memory, and there do I find thee whenever I call thee to memory and delight myself

X, xxiv   in thee.

Animus harps on that it has God in its store, it reassures itself, it re-assures its competence. The soul, however, *anima*, the soul-body notes in this discourse how insistent is the restriction: the Lord is in my memory, concedes the mind, *ex quo didici*

X, xxv   *te*, from the moment that I first learnt thee. So be it, but the soul then asks: where then did I find thee so that I might learn thee? For in my memory

X, xxvi   thou wert not before I learnt thee. Where wert thou, O light, before thou shed light upon me and

kept thyself in me? With steps back and forward, in
the night, we go backward and forward, *et nusquam
locus*, but place there is none, *nusquam locus*,
nowhere the right place. In what place therefore
could I have found thee, that so I might learn thee
and remember thee, in what place, if not in thine
own self, far above myself, *in te supra me?*   Ibid.

Trance

The word is out, in flat denial of *animus*'s plea
for the defense. The *inventio* itself, the encounter
with, the discovery of God does not take place in
the stores of memory. Such apprenticeship exceeds
the mind. Would *anima*, the soul, then, be an angel
that can see God in the light of God, in the heav-
enly part of the heavens, as if it could break
through the heavy vault of the firmament and burst
through the skin of the skies? In what other way
could it have undergone the trial of this appearance? *Animus* declines to write, to describe such an
absurdity, and the mind lays down the *stilus*.

The soul then takes over, and to size up to the

scandal that it is, it lets itself be swept along by song and the thousands-year-old figure of the eastern poetics of love, the *blazon*. Thou calledst and criedst, thou breakdst open my deafness. Thou discoveredst thy beams and hath put my blindness to flight. Thou didst most fragrantly blow upon me, and I pant after thee. I tasted thee, and now do hunger and thirst after thee. Thou didst touch me, X, xxvii and I burned to enjoy thy peace.

In the course of the anamnesis the primal scene is discovered, the violent assault of an encounter: the lost scene of a lost dual, dual scene, dual relation, if it is a relation. Encounter without witness. Unruffled, nonchalance continued to lord it—ordinary pleasures and satisfactions, the daily round of seductions, the vanities of mind. And then, *anima* speaks: you forced entrance into me through my five estuaries, just as the lover excites the five mouths of the woman, swells her lips, those of ear, eye, nose, and tongue, tactile erection swelling from the stomach. Hardly is the soul stunned, consumed by your fire than it is already impatient for the earliest return of your joy, the unnatural peace that the master's fivefold ferocity administers to him.

The Confession of Augustine

The scene is primitive, not locatable in memory.
The absolute eye watched us, Augustine says, he
looked through the lattice of our flesh, he caressed
us with his voice, and we hasten on his scent like
drunk hounds. We believe we take hold of the   XIII, xv
divine, but then, all of a sudden, his calm enrap-
tures us, and uncovered, lashed, outside ourselves,
for one moment we find ourselves gaping in his
beatitude.

The majestic one takes the schoolboy like a
woman, opens him, turns him inside out, turns his
closest intimacy into his shrine, *penetrale meum*, his
shrine in me. The absolute, absolutely irrelative,
outside space and time, so absolutely far—there he
is for one moment lodged in the most intimate part
of this man. Limits are reversed, the inside and the
outside, the before and the after, these miseries of
the mind.

The soul has not penetrated into the angelic
spheres, but a little of the absolute—is it think-
able?—has encrypted itself within it, and the soul
knows nothing of it.

Marked with such a trance, the soul can think of
nothing but of returning to its crimes. A second
offense is neither memory nor repetition, forma-

tion of habit. It is scarcely as if the trace of this trance is retained, since the rules of discourse and sensorial bearings were missing at the moment of its visitation. This trace might be called a fiction, primal, unique, singular and dual, without a third. Be the mind warned, it does not fail to weave around the scene sequences, a story, a biography, the whole calendar of clandestine meetings. The soul is surprised by these inquisitions: how could I know that he is back? I do not know him, I must learn him, he is unknowable.

With a touch, with a fragrance, with his cry, God perhaps (or the devil?) immerses the creature in his presence rather than prizing it therefrom. From the dazed look of daily life, his visit remains hardly discernible, a voice emerging from the next-door garden, the euphoria of a drunk tramp in a street of Milan, Ambrose, his door ajar, reading in silence, his eyes running with too many tears: several clues strewn among habitual signs, almost without our knowing, we poor readers.

He entreats you to help him find them in his own experience. Irrespective of the cruelty of the touch, he has not been distracted in the least from the cares of life, the din of history, the disputes of doctrine. He is even more the son of Adam and of sin, more beholden than ever to responsibilities previously taken on, and all the more fallible, since there is now added to the passions against which he struggles an impetuous ardor whose strident tones, for lack of memory, resonate within him without source.

How could conversion give him light? It exempts him from nothing, it makes everything ring false, the illusory and the true. He prays: But thou, O Lord my God, look upon me, hearken, and behold, and pity and heal me. Thou in whose eyes I am now become a problem to myself, and that is my languor, *ipse est languor meus.* Here lies   X, xxxiii the whole advantage of faith: to become an enigma to oneself, to grow old, hoping for the solution, the resolution from the Other. Have mercy upon me, Yahweh, for I am languishing. Heal me, for my bones are worn.   *Ps.* VI, 2

The condition of use, ontological old age, the delay is that of time upon eternity: O Beauty, I tarried loving you. You were within, but I was outside ... You were with me, but I was not with you. Irreversible handicap. You will have always been ahead of me, I run after you to catch up all this time dissipated outside you. Loss of time, time of loss. My own life is nothing but this: *distensio*, laxity, procrastination.

This delay from which I suffer, of which I am ashamed, that I confess to you, that I attempt, writing my confession, to make up, that I will never make up all the time that I write in time—this delay is but further drawn out by the time of confession, of writing and proclaiming.

Laudes

Indeed the intellect, *animus*, takes up the hand again for the final four lengthy books, the thinker multiplies analysis after analysis, explanation after explanation, allegorical reading after allegorical reading, as if he thought he could have done with the true through discourse—when discourse can do nothing but delay the moment of account.

So night thickens, feebly streaked by the small light of hope. You, the creditor, have left us this hope in pledge, the small *pignus*, this credit over time. And it is considerable: however slender it be, this hope overturns time's course with something like an advance blow, the torsion of tomorrow in today. Listen: for by hope we are already saved, *salvi facti sumus*, hope has made us safe, it has already made of us, children of the night and of the darkness that we were, children of the day and light. Hope does not wait, presence recurs with it, the unbearable light of rapture is there. XIII, xiv

Night, mother of the wicked, will overpass, the wrath of the Lord will overpass, the breath of day will break and the shadows flee. In the morning I shall stand, contemplate, and forever confess unto him . . . Ibid.

Once the body has passed the ordeal of fivefold effraction, standing above, an angel sings his praises. Hope speaks in the future, but now it is morning, daylight comes.

What I am not yet, I am. Its short glow makes us dead to the night of our days. So hope threads a ray of fire in the black web of immanence. What is missing, the absolute, cuts its presence into the shallow furrow of its absence. The fissure that zigzags across the confession spreads with all speed over life, over lives.

The end of the night forever begins.

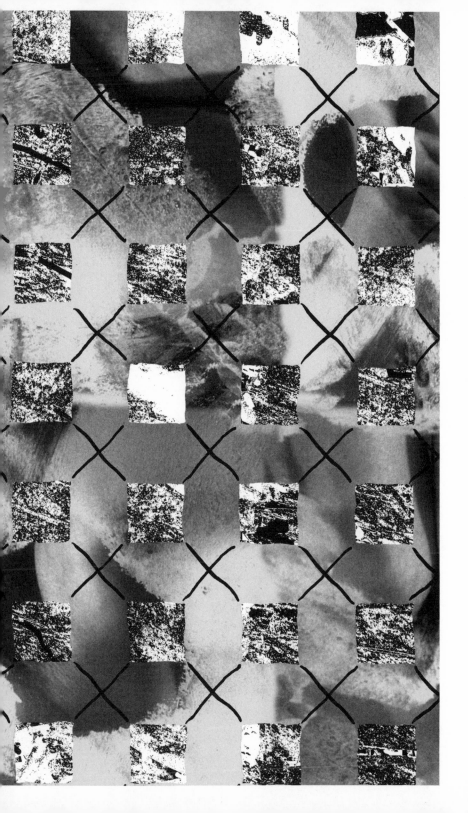

NOTEBOOK

Sendings

Work [*Oeuvre*]

Of whom are the *Confessions* the work, the *opus*? To put it differently, what are they working at, what are they setting into work, and what are they opening up, to what do they open the work?

The opening gives the tone. This tone is a leit-motif, a guiding thread that relentlessly rivets my tone to the order of your omniscience. The introit of the work opens to your presence. This *invocatio*, the voice through which I call upon your voice to come and speak within mine, is repeated through-out the thirteen books, my voice recalls itself to your voice, appeals to it, like a refrain.

My work of confession, of narration and medi-tation, is only my work because it is yours. The life that it recounts, the conversion and the meditation that it relates are the work of your force, your *virtus*. It is your *sapientia*, your knowledge and wisdom, that grants me what I know thereof, as well of what I am ignorant.

Of me, you know everything, having made me in an instant, having established in an instant the plan of my terrestrial journey and my peregrination (my pilgrimage) through the *peripeteia* of events, acts, and passions.

The tone of *invocation* is that of *laudatio*, of praise that the work addresses to its authentic author. The tone is given by a rhythm, which is that of the *Psalms*, the book being quoted profusely in the recurring stream of invocations. The psalm constitutes a song of praise, sung with the harp. The harp is the instrument of the guiding chord, and Augustine is something like the psalmist working the strings, the vibration of which calls forth the voice of the Lord. The psalm rises up, it takes the work out of its immanence, it gathers up its interior transcendence, concealed more deeply than the work can show. The invocation is an act of praise, and this praise is a melody.

The work, before being narration and medita-

tion, is *mélos*, a poem in which the chord of disquiet and that of rest, the chord of death and that
of true life, of question and response send out their
assonant and dissonant vibrations to the address of
the Absolute. Between the narrative moments,
between the meditative moments, where the work
visibly proceeds according to the canons of rhetoric
(the *narratio* constitutes an element of the lawyer's
discourse) and the moments of philosophy (the
meditation, for example, on matter as formlessness,
informitas, owes a lot to Plotinus)—between these
moments, the confession punctuates and suspends
its procedure with invocation, it recalls that this
procedure is *your* procedure, it praises it according
to the (Mideastern) *poetics* of the psalm. The argu-
mentative "disorder," the sequential dissonance of
the questions, to which other questions "respond"
are to be understood foremost as music that the
soul strives to *tune* to the harmony of the involun-
tary divine will, and with which the soul strives to
pay it homage.

"Strives" since this praise is itself placed under
the overall question of the work: who sings your
praise when I sing it? How could the derisory I that
I am, weakest of creatures, even muster within it

the ability to praise you? How could your incommensurability be put into work, even with regard to a poem, into my finitude, how could your atemporality be put into duration, into the *passage* of melody? The very desire to praise you is already your work, and my disquiet (*inquies*) issues from the fact that what is relative is agitated by the absolute. Besides, how could the *invocatio* operate, be satisfied, while it calls you, you the infinite, to come and inhabit me, I who am finite? How could I contain you, how could my work lodge you in the minuscule *place* (*locus*) that I am? In truth, it is the space of my work, a space-time that inhabits the atemporality and aspatiality that you are, this sky that is not of the skies of the earth, but the "sky of the skies, the heaven of the heavens."

To inhabit is still to say too much since the sky of skies is a non-place and a non-time. What my work and my life inhabit, my *bios* and my *graphè* at once, are the mystery of your creation. It is not you, but your *work*, this originary mystery through which, from nowhere and from time immemorial to time immemorial, time and space have been generated. Through the enigma of your appearance and withdrawal, through this "skin" that you have stretched and drawn like a veil between yourself and the world of creatures, you nevertheless diffuse your power and your knowledge. You effuse (*effunderis*) over us; your "presence" in your work, and so in mine, in my life and my book, has neither place nor moment, it is the presence of an *effusion*. You do not disseminate yourself in your creation, you gather it (*collectio*). My *confession* is not only the recital of the gathering of my life under the law of your work, it *is* this recollection that is due to you.

And if, after all, I wonder, as philosophers are wont, how I can know that it is *you* that I invoke, and not some idol, then I can respond that I do not invoke you because I know you, but *so as* to know you. The invocation is a quest and search for you, you who have already found me. After all, if I believe that it is you who are in fact looking for yourself in my confession, it is because you have been preached, and because I believe this *preaching*. *Praedicatus* through the ministry of your son, the preacher who has announced you, speaks in advance. You have wrought through him the *advance* of your presence. My work confesses this advance, strains to be acquitted of it. Its inquest disquiets, its restlessness holds in its advance its *rest*, it rests upon your announced but still concealed presence, it has as its end the quiet of your direct presence, in the sky of skies, the heaven of heavens. It has as its end its own end, the end of works, the vision of the glory: as its end its becoming an angel.

1992

Umbilical of Time

The *Confessions* are written under the temporal sign of waiting. Waiting is the name of the consciousness of the future. But here, because it is a question not only of confessing faith in an end that awaits, that lies in sufferance, but of confessing the self, of displaying the sufferance of what has been done, waiting must go back through the past, climb back to its source, the upstream of this faith, toward the life that has been unhappy, toward the work that it once was.

That which had been promised and which turns waiting into hope is that the work would return to being an *epigraph*. The reversion of writing into the past is demanded by the conversion of what I believed I wrote in your writing. The temporal being that I am can only lend itself to your re-appropriation through the reappropriation of my temporality.

Our body with its weight strives toward its own place. Weight makes not downward only, but to its own place also. The fire mounts upward, a stone sinks downward. . . . My weight is my love; by that am I carried, whithersoever I be carried. We are inflamed by thy gift and are carried upward: we wax hot within, and we go on.   XIII, IX

The past is akin to the below, and love lifts me up toward the above of the future, which is pure quiet. As long as I am not in my place, which is you, restlessness and the impatience of desire are my lot. They are the effects of my own weight. Rememoration makes me run backward, but to do so in order to attain the future that you promise in the very movement of my weight. Things a little out of their place become unquiet, but when they have been put in order again, they are quieted.   IBID.

So takes shape the temporal intrigue, the story of my life. It gives to the succession of events the place that is their due, as facts of my history, in their literal sense. But chronology reduced to itself is pure nothing, appearance and disappearance, passing-away. The past is what is no longer, the future is what is not yet, and the now has no other being than the becoming past of the future. The chase after the future through the past that drives and troubles the *Confessions* is only *possible* if, in the evanescence of these times, something withholds, is maintained, immutable.

The trance of life is this transitivity of finite being. Its literal meaning is non-time, for the "letter" is in itself nonbeing. The plot of confessive narrative is only possible if the event doubles up with another meaning, called "allegorical" by exegesis, if the *opera*, things as they are given, also constitute *signa*. It is conversion, then—since it gives us the ability to read signs in works, to read a little of divine writing in the writing of the *bios*—that justifies confession as a journey that goes backward so as to move forward. The narrative plot, which ties together times in themselves of no import, rises up from a point of time that is not in time, from a point from which time deploys its threefold move to nothingness, but which is itself never destroyed.

It is the exploration of this uncanny anchoring of what happens in what does not pass by that is the concern of the entire end of the *Confessions*. The narrative itself draws to a close at the end of book IX, with the death of Monica, his mother, at Ostia. Nothing on the return to Africa, on the community at Thagaste; then at Hippo, nothing on his hard episcopal life. Hardly a mention of him renouncing the life of a hermit.

The "chase after your voice" comes to an end in book X. Or rather, the chase is pursued in the direction not of the narrative of the past, but of the point from which this narrative is made possible. No longer in the narration of external events, but in the epiphany of the consciousness of time. The agitated movement of things is succeeded by the dizziness of the soul meditating on the peaceful umbilic of this movement, the motif of which will be resumed by Descartes with the *Cogito*. The prose of the world gives place to the poem of memory, or more exactly the phenomenology of internal time. The whole of modern, existential thought on temporality ensues from this meditation: Husserl, Heidegger, Sartre.

The past is no longer, the future is not yet, the present passes by, but as things (*opera*). And yet, I am aware of their nothingness, since I can think them in their absence. There is therefore a present of the past, and this present, as long as I think it, does not pass. It is this present that Husserl will call the *Living Present*, oddly. In Augustine, this present, immanent to internal consciousness, this umbilic, from which signs become readable to me, this present, then, is like the echo in temporality of the divine Present, of his eternal today.

So autobiography (if it is one) changes into cryptography: the last books of the *Confessions* devour this encrypting of the atemporal in the temporal, eat the Word become flesh and single out within the three temporal ecstasies in which it has been sacrificed and, as it were, dispersed, the kernel of permanence in which they are recollected.

1992

Sendings

You [*Toi*]

To guard himself against the endemic pride kindled by the confessive exercise, the confessant has one recourse: to summon you.

A second person indeed hangs over, surveys the *Confessions*, magnetizes them, filters through them. A you, nameless patronym of the catholic community. You is the addressee of the avowal that I write. And yet you is not an interlocutor; you never begins to speak, you never calls me you in turn. I only hear of you from bits of phrases that are reported about your son, about your curses. I invoke you and call you as witness to the purity of my humility: you will never give me quiet, will never acquit me, your jealous love dogs me. My petition leaves you silent. Does it not merit some response? I am only of worth, I exist only through this entreaty, this supplication that is turned toward you, suspended before you. Your silence turns it into a form of torture. But be careful not to take pride in my endurance! May I say that you test me, that you yoke me to the trial of writing this confession in your silence so as to be assured that, wavering on the thread run out between yourself

75

and myself, I do not fall back into the arrogance of being me without you, in my nothingness? If so, you would not only be the addressee of my writing, that to which it is addressed, but also that which gives rise to it, its author.

The suspicion dawns, approaching closer and closer, but very rapidly, that the you, you the silent one, pulls all the strings of the confessive sentence, "carries" all its valences, occupies all the strategic positions, holds them and defends them against any invading conquest. The two poles of the address—addressee and addresser—are both yours, as well as the two poles of meaning—referent and signification. You who remain silent, not me, are the sole concern of the confession, constituting also the content of what is written about it, if to contain and to constitute are permitted terms when what you might signify, under the *stylus* of Augustine, eminently escapes the circumscription of the concept—I was about to say, its inaneness.

You the sole object of the writing and its sole content. If it is true that you thus saturate the entries and exits of the confession, you who confess and you to whom I confess and about which I confess, then I am reduced to receiving nothing but the smallest share. This means little, reduced to nothing, to this nothing which seemed someone, this lure of someone who is no one. I, the apparent subject of the confessive phrase, finds himself, rather loses himself, undone at all ends. And while he confesses his submission to lures, the desire for which continues to rage, while he disavows abject worldliness, he passes under an even more despotic authority, he must accept and savor a quite different radical heteronomy under the law of an unknown master of whom he obstinately delights in making himself the subject.

1997

Fragments

Contretemps

He accuses you. Revealing yourself too late, he complains, you left him all the time to live in ignorance and ignominy. Why did you abandon him? *Eli, Eli, lamma sabactani?* Deprived like David and   *Ps.* XXII, 1 Jesus, orphan of your protection. He caresses in impiety the idea of a life that would have spared him the unhappiness of his life. One in which he would not have had license to stray, extravagant that he is. What was it that I delighted in, but to love and be beloved? . . . Oh, my joy how late came thou! Thou then heldest thy peace, and then wandered I further and further from thee, sowing more sterile seeds of grief, proud in my distress and restless in fatigue.   II, 11

81

Notebook

From the exergue onward he discovers in Paul's
letter to the Romans the tone of anxiety: How shall
they call on him if they do not believe in him? And
Romans X, 14–15   how will they believe without a preacher? But, he
protests, grant me, Lord, to call upon thee in seek-
ing thee, to believe in thee in calling upon thee, for
thou has been preached unto us. What calls upon
thee is the faith which thou hast given me, which
thou hast inspired into me in the humanity of thy
I, 1   Son, and by the ministry of thy preacher. You made
yourself announced, your first fruits inspired in
him the breath that invokes you. Still he calls upon
you without yet knowing you, O wretchedness,
without being able to conjoin with you in the light
of being face to face.

You are ahead of me, I run after you, caught
short by your nimbleness, to recover all this time
dissipated outside you. Much must be endured, so
as to shorten duration; much given out, dispersed,
so as to gather together. He writes on the run to
recover your love, to obtain remission for the evil
times, his hand lifted from the sequestered goods of
pagan origin, forgiveness for heresy.

The confession chokes at this pace. The breath-
less writing in which worldly life is restaged does

not suspend this life's duration, it prolongs and repeats it. To confess the delay redounds to the passive order of delay, and increases it. Even to proclaim that I am yours, I must still be me, only be me. And that you alone are being and the sign, it must still be me who signs the confession.

But who says that it must be? Who, then, is hurrying me on?

Praise

Confiteri, exhomologesthai, the Septuagint says, to recognize one's errors in front of a witness, to proclaim them. To glorify the Impeccable: Confession is not only about admitting one's faults, it is also about praising. . . . There is a confession of praise.

The *laudatio* of the pagans flatters the dead person, makes of him an example, celebrates his merits. But it also pities him wandering in the underworld, far from his loved ones, it calls him back to the sensible sun. Remain with us, the living, be eternal in the light of immanence!

In the Psalms of David, the complaint is turned

Enarr. in Ps. CXLV, 13

83

upside down, the beyond becomes more real than this world. You are the only life, O Lord the invisible, and the only power, and I, your people here, owe my survival alone to your protection. For I am encircled by the enemy, threatened with nothing, persecuted, weak from within. Never shall I obey

IX, IV   you enough, never shall I be just enough to deserve you. Command, forgive.

You elected me to give reign to your law in the world and myself, and you know me unworthy of such ministry. Show mercy upon my efforts.

To celebrate the *virtus* and the *sapientia* of the master is the way for the servant to admit his own lowliness: incomparable beings. Great art thou, O Lord, and greatly to be praised; great is thy force and

IBID.   innumerable is thy wisdom. What we hear at the very beginning of the *Confessions* is a psalm of *tehillâh*, David's, Psalm CXLV, the alleluia praising your glory.

Psalmody

Throughout the thirteen books he lifts whole verses from the psalmist. As recitatives accompanied by strings, poems in parallel hemistiches whose balance sometimes is broken with the rhythm of the *quînâh*, the short litanies move the body in minimal choreographic figures; one limps in jerks so as to deplore the infirmity of being unable to walk straight, offering this infirmity up. Savors, exhalations of flesh, touches of sound and gesture that make the blood of the community throb—a whole life astray comes with the psalmody to beat the holy meditation, the wise argumentation, the upright narrative, to interrupt the clear string of thoughts and tie it to the other, the red and black fiber of flesh, through which evil holds the creature in its darkness, through which it comes to pass that divine lightning sets him afire. The fabric of the *Confessions* is closely knitted, thread upon thread, as inextricable as the nature of David and Christ, sometimes with thought following the carnal rhythm of call and abandonment to be consumed in unison for a communal feast, and sometimes, the flesh placed to one side, with the *stilus* passing into the firm hand of discourse that reasons, that recounts, that teaches for the sake of another body, that of the lovers of Annunciation, true catholic readers. X, xxix

What cries, *voces*, I gave unto thee, my God, while I read the Psalms of David; these faithful songs, those sounds of piety! . . . Oh, what cries made I unto thee with and in those Psalms! Oh, how was I inflamed toward thee by them! Yea, I was on fire to have resounded them, had I been able, in X, IV all the world, against the pride of mankind.

There is the whole book for lack of this world, or in its place there vibrates an ancient rumor, born from the oldest East and millennial Egypt, passing through the Hebrews to the Western churches, the psalmody in which sobs the abandonment to nothingness and rises up gratitude to God for his help. Lamentable repetition, exaltation. When I called upon thee, thou heardest me, god of my righteous-IBID. ness, thou hast enlarged me in my distress. With the same breath the voice shivers with fear and burns with hope.

Fissure

Antiphons, confessions, responsorials as much as psalms: the fissure runs between waiting and anxi-

ety, a most shallow furrow that is irreparable for
ages, before the soul's reunion with itself in death
before God. Until then, the uncertainty that is faith
must be woven, one must knot together the two
strands that God's incision in the tessitura of the
soul had undone: the soul still belongs to the self, it
already belongs to God. Pain and joy. And therefore
threatened by two sins: either the I reveling in its
own distress, or assuming to fawn upon the good
lord to prize salvation out of him. The show of
suffering, the bragging of praise. How can this creature find the right tone unless God helps him? But
how shall it know that he is helping unless his signs
are decipherable? If, indeed, it is still right to attrib-
ute the trances to his love, and not, perhaps, to a
cunning error, thereby putting them out of account.

For God also tempts the soul, as if he was fond
of proving its weaknesses rather than kindling its
virtue. The imprint that he has stamped into it,
almost by surprise, and that leaves it divided within
itself, exerts such influence that the soul continues
to sigh for the return of ecstasy, henceforth devoted
to this visiting and condemned to repetition like a
sinner slave to his or her worst inclinations. Carry
me away, convey me hither, set ablaze, subvert!   X, xxix

Pencil Sketch

Sin

*To confess in writing, through writing, to write
out sin and obedience instead of confiding them to
the inclined, immediate ear of the authorized priest
or of the community living under the law: how does
the confession of wrong and the request for forgiveness merit credence if their formulation has called
for negotiation with language, bargaining—little
matters whether it be long or short: whatever, it is
treacherous and perverse—with the already said
from which the written word ensues?*

*As soon as terror, love, that is, prayer have been
brought under the written word, we sense that they
have been affected. All the more so if the tones that
the orant, the confessant presses upon his or her*

writing endeavor to be equal to the cries of the sup-
plicants, the sighs that delay the inadmissible, each
choking of shame, the guttural timbres that clothe
self-hatred and self-indulgence. Never as much, per-
haps, as in confession does the art of writing appear
more out of place, more sham, more astray. One
waits for panting words, hot off the breath, almost
disgusting in pitch. Sin must be vomited out in
spasms. Its confession will be seen as genuine only
insofar as it is irrepressible, as if confession in itself
was already due to the grace of the power it invokes,
making the sinner unable to keep within his or her
ignominy.

   Sin is silence, it hides from the communal rule of
conversation, of friendship its villainy. It holds in
check words inclined to actions, separates, dissoci-
ates. Confession discharges the villainy that has been
amassed in secret. It turns into words, verba facit,
things that have been committed, res actae. *It is*
agreed that speaking can relieve. Whereas writing is
an exercise, from which ensues a work which is not
called upon to be sincere. The letter is not moved by
the energy of having had enough, it precisely can, it
can still defer expression, seek and choose its terms.
In writing the thing is not hated, it is not excreted,

*it arranges its signs, money the general equivalent of
[. . .] Nothing is less trustworthy than signs. They
coldly defer meaning, they also fall silent, out of
excess, the overflowing abundance for which they
can be exchanged; they can substitute for anything,
they want nothing. It is up to the reader to guess the*
res *that they are presumed to signify; thus he or she
discovers, that is, reinvents the thing. The reader
bestows tone upon dead letters. In short, as the timbre sets meaning, the voice alone guarantees the confession. Written, confession constitutes a duty, a* pen-
sum *demanded by authority, a formula within the
rules, an act drawn up in law that will be used later
to exonerate or incriminate the confessant.*

*The young lady from Ascoli Piceno who passes by,
kneels her troubled body at the sliding wooden grid
behind which the indiscreet snout of a monk, that
she will have never seen, surveys intently; she serves
him up the broad outlines of her shameful day-
dreaming, she stands up blessed with his ten Ave, to
be recited immediately against a pillar of the cathe-
dral. She confesses and will have confessed. Speed of
decision, slenderness of avowal, intrepid quavering
in the voice—they vouch for the fact that she will
not have lied, that she did not give herself the time*

to travesty. If God forgives, she will hear it before penitence is over. She is certain that God will not dawdle. He recognizes the truth in the very moment that, with one stroke, she strips off the sedimented layers of her silence. Under the soft, modest, short, impassive voice, the devil of the written word, of the already written retracts, folds up its baggage of words and obscene idols that mutter aside.

The Marchesiana now runs onto the high piazza, smooth like her soul, [. . .] toward the life that begins, her life does not stop beginning, she inhales with her whole bosom the munificent ruddiness of the evening sky, lying with all its weight on the sea's edge. The view of Ascoli Piceno reaches easily as far as the east shore when the weather is as pure as a girl's face. She is forgiven, she confesses just to tempt God, to see if that evil thought that glided through her body like a swift would have amused God. Her arms round under her mantilla send out a warm, beige landscape in liturgical response to the rising freshness that ascends between the pines and the cypresses. A smooth child is this landscape that begins and has never sinned. Nothing is more holy than its lightness. The night of confessional serves to make hoarse the shame of large male infamies. But

Pencil Sketch

God delights in the light hue [. . .] the virgin clar-inets.

But then, in the end, tablet after tablet heaped up by the old prelate of Hippo to give detailed evi-dence of his wrongdoings does not particularly please the lord, it [. . .] scares. Like a dossier for prosecu-tion. Not only because these confessions make it clear to what extent his creatures have been poorly put together to be so unhappy, but also because he finds out to what perverse use writing can be turned, when it has been given to them by him. The holy man will make a point, line after line, of men-tioning everything that displeased, he will bring all possible evidence to his case, will cudgel his memory not to forget the slightest detail: one tear too many, a gratuitous theft, an excessive liking for church songs. He summons the very silence and caprices of his childhood. It is imperative that, after the labori-ous report, every single thing that he believes merits the lord's indignation is recorded.

This is a testament upside down, it is not the covenant of one voice with another, not a gift of words: here is what you owe, and as a result you will have my protection. The promise has passed, the accounts are to be drawn up. There remain the writings of the spoken word, to these writings respond what spoke in Augustine's life, together with which he mentions failures of memory, lapses. He, the bishop, has nothing to bequeath but his sins. Is it possible—the divine solicitor, the judge wonders— is it really possible for his life to have ended in such a negative slate? What game is he playing with me, pleading one hundred percent guilty? Trying to snatch some sympathy from me.

Fac-similes

confèrence lip

1ères pages du livre

La Confession

pas de confession qui n'exige un
début de conversion. Conversion
celle ... les circonstances
des ... et ordinaires à une
... mutation, les circonstances
de l'adresse avant tout. La
... frappe / le corps ...
... dans ses 5 sens.
... Titre de refus. :
les confessions de l'A.

Titre du livre :
Augustin, le bon usage de l'amenuise.
Le phase intitulée (rhétorique, ...
argumentaire, persuasion) travaille
en défaut se rapporte à l'acuité de la
tentative, et tentation d'ajoud encore,
tout par le phase-effort ne surgit pas de
se violence d'obscuri d'absurde inassignable
et s'erige par la proximité du qu'od
vous avant le point. A partir du
choix de la rencontre, La confession
s'engage de l'immensité du pouvoir
transposant, mais c'est pour verser
se fracturer au profit d'une cité
future, d'une église.

Séminaire 1

X nov 38   Blason : les 5 sens = le corps ouvert / fermé
                      la violence, effraction : (= tu arrives, je disparais

→ Duplicité de th. écriture ?

Sommaire 2

Confusion des voix
 - des *le* et *la*
 - des temps
 - des *sexes*.

Cette confusion ou ces confusions ~~relèvent~~ ~~des~~
résultent un différend
 c'est à dire : ce n'est pas seulement
  1. ni des croisements de "lignes de voix" ou
   de temps ou d'espace hétérogènes
   croisements de le monde
            sur la langue   l'A.
           ou le verbe
  Il serait alors un nom pour une
  foule de ... *ça* ou d'intensités
  hétérogènes mes fortuitement de rencontre

  2. ni la confusion ~~comme~~ prendre ... ~~oui~~ ou
   du nom dans le moment négatif dialectique.
   ~~...~~ Type : il fallait que Janus fût offensé
   et brouillé pour que sa gloire se révèle.

 - Peut-être le confort Type : eh bien justement pour ça !
               Objection : il est mensonge ... ?
                      détruit.
   ~~...~~ que ça ne fait
   pas dialectique, ~~et~~ mais
   renvoi infini du oui au non
   et non au oui = Individualité

 Individualité manifeste de l'inde des ...,
  des actions et des signes
  ~~...~~ qu'une indétermination ... toujours autres
  du un même
  mais le ~~...~~ cohérence ... de ... voir
  qui parlant d'un objet et sous un seul ...
  ... ... des choses incompatibles.
  c'est p... une affaire de ton   encore

 Noter une chose importante :
  cette individualité est-elle perdue dès lors que le
  langage s'écrit et qu'elle ... ... silencieusement ?
  On en contraire la neutralité apparente du
  timbre des phrases lues en silence ... + elle mieux
  paraître l'individualité de leur sens ?
         Interpréter sera décider ? Souvent. Mais
  ne peut-être aussi trouver le ton de l'indécidable,
  cela existe-t-il ? Rapport avec le ton faux

Lab 186
Comme moi ... je
vendais l'art de
bien parler

Sommaire 3

Explication au sens ... à haute voix, jouer le texte,
c'est le ~~...~~ faire pour un corps,
le faire chair, l'incarner.

Comment dire que le texte s'incarne ... n'a pas
le texte lu en silence ? On ... et incarnation
favorise le postiche, le mensonge germanique, etc
(Rome / Luther). ... Rameau, surtout Paradoxe
comédien : le gestus de l'écriture A, son brillon-
nement, à proportion du flegme, de l'inertie de
l'âme — grand ami, pas d'émoi.

Texte lu ... vive voix, comédie, improvisé en
1ère instance, mais chanté et danté c. Psaumes
miment ... ou plainte ——

Lecture silencieuse : Ambroise comprise contre la
comédie des pleurs et des entrechats ?

Au moment inversion
~~...~~ audio vocem canta dicentis —
et cretro repetentis
quasi pueri an puellae:
Tolle lege ; tolle lege

À commenter par ... d'Antoine
... réf. Lab 200 lignes 11 à 7
avec les 2 propositions
— tanquam sibi directum quod legebatur
— et tali oraculo confestim ad ~~...~~ esse
conversum

Et quel est le verset foudroyant ?
Matthieu XIX, 21
(Vade, vende omnia, quae habes, da pauperibus
et habebis thesaurum in caelis, et veni,
sequere me

... de ce point ... était
lu à son intention

il faut par un oracle ...
sigmum, convertit à toi ... le drame

va, vend tout ... que tu as
donne le aux pauvres ...
... tu l'amasse des trésors
... prieras et suis moi

cf VIII vii 18
quo audacior milii

Vois tu, préfère moi à tout, le vrai trésor
est au ciel. ...
Suis moi. ... tibi ... à moi.
... un génie de toi

Convertir; on ne le sera jamais assez, on n'en
sera jamais assuré et tranquille. Parce que la
conversion véritable ne peut se dire vraiment
vraiment, en vérité, que d'un instant comme
d'une vision : l'apparition d'un visage au flanc
d'un mur ou le chant d'une voix dans
d'un silence des arbres : alors par cette énigme
brille le corps qui appelle et s'appelle d'être
à déchiffrer. Or elle ne déchiffre rien,
elle ne laisse trouver, elle brille et
jouit. Mais ça ne dure pas. Alors ils
se rappellent, l'âme et le corps, ils se
tournent le visage où la voix est se
lamentent.

La conversion périt sur sa précarité. Ah
s'installer dans sa foi au cœur
du silence au lieux, me priver du mur

Cultural Memory | in the Present